Useful cooking conversi...

WEIGHT

Ounce (oz) = 28.349 grams (g)
Gram = 0.035 ounces
Pound (lb) = 0.454 kilograms (kg)
Kilogram = 2.205 pounds

LENGTH

Inch (in) = 25.4 millimetres (mm)
Millimetre = 0.039 inches
Inch = 2.54 centimetres (cm)
Centimetre = 0.394 inches

AREA

Square inch = 645.2 square millimetres
Square millimetre (sq mm) = 0.0016 square inches (sq in)
Square centimetre (sq cm) = 0.155 square inches
Square inch (sq in) = 6.452 square centimetres

CAPACITY

Pint = 0.568 litres
Litre = 1.760 pints
Imp. Gallon = 4.546 litres
Litre = 0.220 Imp gallon
Pint = 20 fluid ounces (fl oz)
Millilitre (ml) = 0.035 fluid ounces
Fluid ounces = 28.413 millilitres
Teaspoon (tsp) = 5 millilitres
Dessertspoon (dsp) = 10 millilitres
Tablespoon (tbsp) = 15 millilitres
Cup = 140 millilitres

Note: American teaspoon = dessertspoon

RACHEL ALLEN

Rachel's
Diary
2008

Collins

Personal notes

NAME:

ADDRESS:

TELEPHONE:

MOBILE:

E-MAIL:

BUSINESS TELEPHONE:

BUSINESS ADDRESS:

2008 at a glance

	January	February	March	April	May	June
Mon						
Tue	1			1		
Wed	2			2		
Thur	3			3	1	
Fri	4	1		4	2	
Sat	5	2	1	5	3	
Sun	6	3	2	6	4	1
Mon	7	4	3	7	5	2
Tue	8	5	4	8	6	3
Wed	9	6	5	9	7	4
Thur	10	7	6	10	8	5
Fri	11	8	7	11	9	6
Sat	12	9	8	12	10	7
Sun	13	10	9	13	11	8
Mon	14	11	10	14	12	9
Tue	15	12	11	15	13	10
Wed	16	13	12	16	14	11
Thur	17	14	13	17	15	12
Fri	18	15	14	18	16	13
Sat	19	16	15	19	17	14
Sun	20	17	16	20	18	15
Mon	21	18	17	21	19	16
Tue	22	19	18	22	20	17
Wed	23	20	19	23	21	18
Thur	24	21	20	24	22	19
Fri	25	22	21	25	23	20
Sat	26	23	22	26	24	21
Sun	27	24	23	27	25	22
Mon	28	25	24	28	26	23
Tue	29	26	25	29	27	24
Wed	30	27	26	30	28	25
Thur	31	28	27		29	26
Fri		29	28		30	27
Sat			29		31	28
Sun			30			29
Mon			31			30
Tue						

July	August	September	October	November	December	
		1			1	Mon
1		2			2	Tue
2		3	1		3	Wed
3		4	2		4	Thur
4	1	5	3		5	Fri
5	2	6	4	1	6	Sat
6	3	7	5	2	7	Sun
7	4	8	6	3	8	Mon
8	5	9	7	4	9	Tue
9	6	10	8	5	10	Wed
10	7	11	9	6	11	Thur
11	8	12	10	7	12	Fri
12	9	13	11	8	13	Sat
13	10	14	12	9	14	Sun
14	11	15	13	10	15	Mon
15	12	16	14	11	16	Tue
16	13	17	15	12	17	Wed
17	14	18	16	13	18	Thur
18	15	19	17	14	19	Fri
19	16	20	18	15	20	Sat
20	17	21	19	16	21	Sun
21	18	22	20	17	22	Mon
22	19	23	21	18	23	Tue
23	20	24	22	19	24	Wed
24	21	25	23	20	25	Thur
25	22	26	24	21	26	Fri
26	23	27	25	22	27	Sat
27	24	28	26	23	28	Sun
28	25	29	27	24	29	Mon
29	26	30	28	25	30	Tue
30	27		29	26	31	Wed
31	28		30	27		Thur
	29		31	28		Fri
	30			29		Sat
	31			30		Sun
						Mon
						Tue

Introduction

Welcome to 2008! I love the start of a new year; it's the perfect opportunity to contemplate all the glorious dishes to create throughout the seasons and the fun I'll have preparing them. Of course, like you, I also aim to turn over a new leaf and get really organised this year!

My desk diary will lend a helping hand in planning your busy life; whether you're juggling work commitments, quality time with the family, a jam-packed social life, or, most likely, all of the above. Remember too that so much of life is about the joys of delicious food, so this diary is also a celebration of seasonal ingredients and scrumptious holiday treats.

Keep this little book by your side throughout the year and find inspiration to get creative in the kitchen. Each month is introduced with mouth-watering seasonal ideas or tasty ways to enjoy a special occasion. You'll also find imaginative suggestions and culinary tips to help all your cooking run smoothly. Every month features an easy-to-follow recipe that perfectly complements the time of year. Don't forget, you can also jot down all your own culinary ideas in the recipe notes section at the back.

So, join me for a year of celebrating seasonal food and cooking!

Rachel x

January

Start the new year with a healthy detox! Fresh fruit and vegetable smoothies or juices are packed with vitamins and absolutely scrumptious. Whiz up some chopped ginger for added zing, or throw in a handful of oats for slow-releasing carbohydrates.

DECEMBER JANUARY 2008

31 MONDAY

01 TUESDAY New Year's Day

02 WEDNESDAY Public Holiday, Scotland

03 THURSDAY

04 FRIDAY

05 SATURDAY

06 SUNDAY

WK	M	T	W	T	F	S	S
1		1	2	3	4	5	6
2	7	8	9	10	11	12	13
3	14	15	16	17	18	19	20
4	21	22	23	24	24	26	27
5	28	29	30	31			

JANUARY 2008

07 MONDAY

08 TUESDAY ◉ New Moon

09 WEDNESDAY

10 THURSDAY

11 FRIDAY

12 SATURDAY

13 SUNDAY

♡ **Start the day off with a big bowl of porridge.
It is low GI and perfect for keeping you full
of energy until lunch.**

JANUARY 2008

14 MONDAY

15 TUESDAY

16 WEDNESDAY

17 THURSDAY

18 FRIDAY

19 SATURDAY

20 SUNDAY

Wholewheat Loaf with Oats and Seeds

I love this healthy, nutty brown bread, it keeps very nice and fresh for a couple of days, then after that it's delicious toasted.

MAKES ONE 2LB LOAF

200g (7oz) wholewheat flour
75g (3oz) plain flour
75g (3oz) mixture of sesame, poppy and sunflower seeds,
   plus 2 tbsp for scattering over the top
50g (2oz) oats
25g (1oz) bran
1 tsp salt
350–400ml (12–14fl oz) warm water
1 tbsp honey (or treacle or molasses)
15g (1/2oz) fresh yeast or 1 x 7g (1/4oz) sachet dried yeast
1 tbsp sunflower oil

1. Preheat the oven to 200°C (400°F), Gas mark 6. Line or grease a 900g (2lb) loaf tin.

2. In a large bowl, mix the flours, seeds (except those reserved for scattering), oats, bran and salt. Place 100ml (3 1/2fl oz) of the water in a measuring jug, stir in the honey, then sprinkle in the yeast. Leave for about 5 minutes until frothy (fresh yeast will be more frothy than dried yeast). Add all of the remaining water except for 60ml (2fl oz) and sunflower oil and mix.

3. Pour into the dry ingredients and mix well. The mixture should be wet and sloppy, but if it's not, add the remaining 60ml (2fl oz) of warm water. Turn into the loaf tin and sprinkle over the reserved seeds. Cover with a light tea towel or napkin and leave in a warm place until risen to the top of the tin. Remove the tea towel and bake in the oven for 1 hour.

4. When you think it's cooked, remove the bread from the tin and check to see if it is – if it sounds hollow when you tap it on the bottom of the loaf then it's cooked. If it's not cooked, put it back in the oven without the tin for another 5–10 minutes. Cool on a wire rack.

JANUARY 2008

21 MONDAY

22 TUESDAY ○ Full Moon

23 WEDNESDAY

24 THURSDAY

25 FRIDAY

26 SATURDAY

27 SUNDAY

WK	M	T	W	T	F	S	S
1		1	2	3	4	5	6
2	7	8	9	10	11	12	13
3	14	15	16	17	18	19	20
4	21	22	23	24	24	26	27
5	28	29	30	31			

JANUARY FEBRUARY 2008

28 **MONDAY** Australia Day

29 TUESDAY

30 WEDNESDAY

31 THURSDAY

01 FRIDAY

02 SATURDAY

03 SUNDAY

♡ Leeks are at their best at this time of year. Add them to a potato gratin or a wholesome soup for a warming seasonal dinner.

February

Rich, dark, hot chocolate really is comfort in a cup. Serve with marshmallows and cinnamon or a dash of brandy, for an indulgent St Valentine's Day treat.

FEBRUARY 2008

04 **MONDAY**

05 **TUESDAY**

06 **WEDNESDAY** Waitangi Day, NZ

07 **THURSDAY** ● New Moon | Chinese New Year

08 **FRIDAY**

09 **SATURDAY**

10 **SUNDAY**

WK	M	T	W	T	F	S	S
5					1	2	3
6	4	5	6	7	8	9	10
7	11	12	13	14	15	16	17
8	18	19	20	21	22	23	24
9	25	26	27	28	29		

11 **MONDAY** National Foundation Day, Japan

12 **TUESDAY**

13 **WEDNESDAY**

14 **THURSDAY** St Valentine's Day

15 **FRIDAY**

16 **SATURDAY**

17 **SUNDAY**

♡ **Leave a plate of heart-shaped biscuits on your loved-one's pillow for a Valentine's treat.**

Chocolate Melting Moments

I absolutely adore these little Australian melt-in-the-mouth treats.
They make a perfect dessert to share with your loved one!

MAKES 24 HALVES (12 WHEN SANDWICHED TOGETHER)
125g (4¹/₂oz) butter, softened
50g (2oz) icing sugar
50g (2oz) cornflour
25g (1oz) cocoa powder
100g (4oz) plain flour
about 2 tbsp chocolate hazelnut spread

1. Preheat the oven to 180°C/350°F/Gas mark 3 and lightly grease
or line a baking tray with parchment paper.
2. Beat the butter, then add the icing sugar and beat until soft and
light. Sift the cornflour, cocoa powder and plain flour into the butter
and sugar and mix until the dough comes together.
3. Divide the dough into 24 equal parts (about the size of a walnut in
its shell). Roll into balls, place slightly apart on the prepared tray and
then flatten each biscuit lightly with a fork. Cook in the preheated
oven for 10–12 minutes or until firm. Remove from the oven and let
the biscuits sit on the tray for 5 minutes before transferring to a wire
rack to cool. Then sandwich the biscuits together with a nice thick
layer of chocolate hazelnut spread.

18 MONDAY

19 TUESDAY

20 WEDNESDAY

21 THURSDAY ○ Full Moon

22 FRIDAY

23 SATURDAY

24 SUNDAY

WK	M	T	W	T	F	S	S
5					1	2	3
6	4	5	6	7	8	9	10
7	11	12	13	14	15	16	17
8	18	19	20	21	22	23	24
9	25	26	27	28	29		

FEBRUARY MARCH 2008

25 MONDAY

26 TUESDAY

27 WEDNESDAY

28 THURSDAY

29 FRIDAY

01 SATURDAY St. David's Day

02 SUNDAY Mothering Sunday

Dark green cabbage is so good for you as it's packed
with vitamin C. Try it sautéed rather than boiled
to keep its goodness.

March

An edible gift is a lovely way to say 'thank you' on Mothering Sunday. Why not bake a classic Victoria sponge cake, or cut homemade shortbread into cute shapes. These ideas are great for children to help with, too.

MARCH 2008

03 MONDAY

04 TUESDAY

05 WEDNESDAY

06 THURSDAY

07 FRIDAY ● New Moon

08 SATURDAY

09 SUNDAY

WK	M	T	W	T	F	S	S
9						1	2
10	3	4	5	6	7	8	9
11	10	11	12	13	14	15	16
12	17	18	19	20	21	22	23
13	24	25	26	27	28	29	30
14	31						

10 MONDAY Commonwealth Day

11 TUESDAY

12 WEDNESDAY

13 THURSDAY

14 FRIDAY

15 SATURDAY

16 SUNDAY

For a St Patrick's Day starter make a delicious
green soup with spinach, watercress or peas.

Thai Peanut, Vegetable and Coconut Noodles

I love this quick, delicious noodle dish, it is so warming and filling, yet not too heavy. Perfect for the spring weather!

SERVES 4

1 x 400ml tin of coconut milk
1 tbsp sunflower or peanut oil
2 tbsp red curry paste
3 tbsp crunchy peanut butter
300ml (½ pint) vegetable stock
3–4 tbsp fish sauce
1 tbsp brown sugar
250g (9oz) medium rice noodles
150g (5oz) baby corn cobs, cut into slices at an angle
150g (5oz) broccoli, cut into small florets
150g (5oz) mange tout, cut in half at an angle
50g (2oz) spring onion, trimmed and sliced into strips and dropped
    into a bowl of iced water to curl
100g (4oz) toasted peanuts, roughly chopped
2 tbsp torn fresh basil or roughly chopped fresh coriander

1. Heat a wok or large wide pan, add the oil, then the coconut milk (if it has separated, set aside the watery part first). Stir over a high heat until the coconut milk starts to separate and thicken.
2. Add the curry paste and the peanut butter and mix, then add the stock, fish sauce and sugar and bring to the boil.
3. Meanwhile, place the noodles in a bowl and cover with boiling water, leave for 5 minutes to soften before draining and rinsing with water to prevent them sticking.
4. Add the corn and the broccoli to the pan and cook, uncovered, for a minute then add the mange tout and spring onion, and cook for another 1–2 minutes. Stir in half the chopped peanuts and half the herbs and taste, adding more fish sauce if you want it to be salty.
5. Add the drained noodles and toss to mix. Place in a large warm serving bowl, or individual bowls, then scatter with the remaining peanuts and herbs before serving.

MARCH 2008

17 **MONDAY** St. Patrick's Day

18 **TUESDAY**

19 **WEDNESDAY**

20 **THURSDAY**

21 **FRIDAY** ○ Full Moon | Good Friday

22 **SATURDAY**

23 **SUNDAY**

WK	M	T	W	T	F	S	S
9						1	2
10	3	4	5	6	7	8	9
11	10	11	12	13	14	15	16
12	17	18	19	20	21	22	23
13	24	25	26	27	28	29	30
14	31						

24 MONDAY Easter Monday

25 TUESDAY

26 WEDNESDAY

27 THURSDAY

28 FRIDAY

29 SATURDAY

30 SUNDAY British Summer Time Begins

♡ Enjoy purple sprouting broccoli at this time
of year as a delicious, healthy side-dish.

April

Spinach is an essential spring-time super-food as it's loaded with nutrients like iron and calcium. It's perfect in a salad, added to cheese quesadillas or packed into a warm frittata.

MARCH APRIL 2008

31 MONDAY

01 TUESDAY

02 WEDNESDAY

03 THURSDAY

04 FRIDAY

05 SATURDAY

06 SUNDAY ⊘ New Moon

WK	M	T	W	T	F	S	S
14		1	2	3	4	5	6
15	7	8	9	10	11	12	13
16	14	15	16	17	18	19	20
17	21	22	23	24	24	26	27
18	28	29	30				

07 MONDAY

08 TUESDAY

09 WEDNESDAY

10 THURSDAY

11 FRIDAY

12 SATURDAY

13 SUNDAY

♡ Watercress is so nutritious and in season right now. Great in soups and salads, or try in place of basil for a gorgeous, unusual pesto.

Rhubarb Muffins

Rhubarb is at its best at this time of year. These delicious muffins work perfectly for breakfast, or as a snack at any time of day!

MAKES 10 LARGE MUFFINS
125g (5oz) light brown sugar
15ml (1tb sp) sunflower oil
1 egg
1 tsp vanilla extract
100ml (3½fl oz) buttermilk
100g (4oz) rhubarb, finely diced
175g (6oz) plain flour
1 level tsp baking powder
1 level tsp bicarbonate of soda
Pinch of salt

FOR THE TOPPING
25g (1oz) light Muscovado sugar

1. Preheat the oven to 200°C (400°F), Gas mark 6. Place 10 paper muffin cases in a muffin tray.
2. Place the sugar, oil, egg, vanilla extract and buttermilk in a large bowl. Beat until well mixed. Add the rhubarb and mix. Sift in the flour, baking powder, bicarbonate of soda and salt, and stir until all the ingredients are mixed. Do not over-stir.
3. Fill the muffin cases three-quarters full with batter. Leave to chill and sprinkle the Muscovado sugar on top of the batter in each muffin case.
4. Bake in the oven on the centre shelf for 18–20 minutes until golden brown. Cool on a wire rack.

APRIL 2008

14 MONDAY

15 TUESDAY

16 WEDNESDAY

17 THURSDAY

18 FRIDAY

19 SATURDAY

20 SUNDAY ○ Full Moon

WK	M	T	W	T	F	S	S
14		1	2	3	4	5	6
15	7	8	9	10	11	12	13
16	14	15	16	17	18	19	20
17	21	22	23	24	24	26	27
18	28	29	30				

APRIL 2008

21 MONDAY

22 TUESDAY

23 WEDNESDAY St. George's Day

24 THURSDAY

25 FRIDAY Anzac Day

26 SATURDAY

27 SUNDAY

♡ **Stock up on fresh rhubarb now, slice and freeze for delicious year-round rhubarb fools, crumbles and pies.**

May

Asparagus is at its seasonal best in late spring. It tastes great in pasta, risotto and tarts. Or drizzle with gorgeous home-made hollandaise sauce – the ideal accompaniment to a cold glass of white wine!

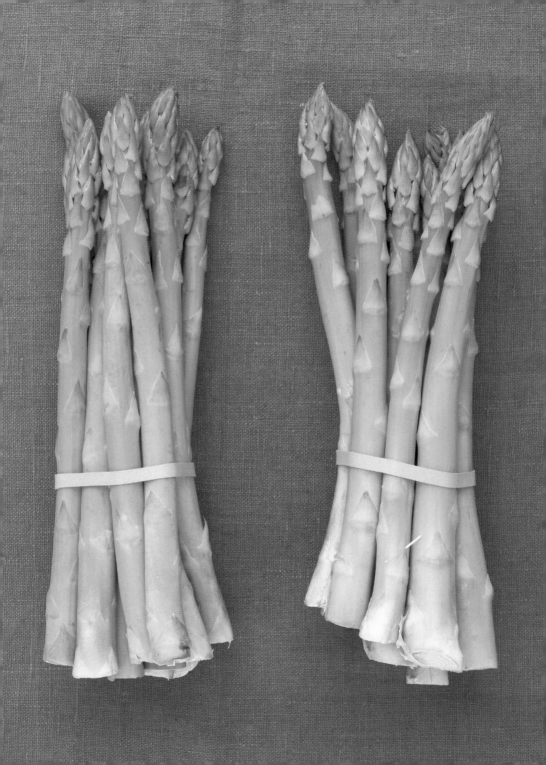

APRIL MAY 2008

28 MONDAY

29 TUESDAY

30 WEDNESDAY

01 THURSDAY

02 FRIDAY

03 SATURDAY

04 SUNDAY

WK	M	T	W	T	F	S	S
18				1	2	3	4
19	5	6	7	8	9	10	11
20	12	13	14	15	16	17	18
21	19	20	21	22	23	24	25
22	26	27	28	29	30	31	

05 **MONDAY** ● New Moon | May Day Holiday, UK & R. of Ireland

06 **TUESDAY**

07 **WEDNESDAY**

08 **THURSDAY**

09 **FRIDAY**

10 **SATURDAY**

11 **SUNDAY**

Enjoy the first of the new potatoes now; place a couple of sprigs of mint and a good pinch of salt in the water when boiling for added flavour.

MAY 2008

12 MONDAY

13 TUESDAY

14 WEDNESDAY

15 THURSDAY

16 FRIDAY

17 SATURDAY

18 SUNDAY

Prawns with Lemon Mayonnaise

One of the best ways to enjoy freshly cooked prawns is to serve them with a homemade mayonnaise and some crusty bread.

SERVES 4

FOR THE LEMON MAYONNAISE:
2 egg yolks
A pinch of salt
1/2 tsp Dijon mustard
1 tbsp lemon juice
225ml (8fl oz) oil (I like to use 200ml sunflower oil and 25ml olive oil)
1-2 tsp chopped tarragon and chives

FOR THE PRAWNS:
About 28 large prawns
Dash olive oil

TO SERVE:
Crusty white or brown bread

1. First make the lemon mayonnaise. Put the egg yolks in a non-metallic bowl, add the salt, mustard and lemon juice and mix well.

2. Add the oil gradually, just a drop at a time, whisking continuously.

3. You should start to see the mixture thickening, keep adding the oil as you whisk.

4. Add the chopped herbs, stir and season to taste. Refrigerate until ready to serve.

5. To cook the prawns, pre-heat the olive oil in a large frying pan on a high heat.

6. Add the prawns and toss them in the olive oil for 2-3 minutes until cooked through to the centre. When they are cooked they will be firm and white. Very large ones may take 30 seconds to 1 minute more.

7. Serve with the mayonnaise drizzled on top and the fresh bread on the side.

19 MONDAY

20 TUESDAY ○ Full Moon

21 WEDNESDAY

22 THURSDAY

23 FRIDAY

24 SATURDAY

25 SUNDAY

WK	M	T	W	T	F	S	S
18				1	2	3	4
19	5	6	7	8	9	10	11
20	12	13	14	15	16	17	18
21	19	20	21	22	23	24	25
22	26	27	28	29	30	31	

26 **MONDAY** Spring Holiday, UK

27 **TUESDAY**

28 **WEDNESDAY**

29 **THURSDAY**

30 **FRIDAY**

31 **SATURDAY**

01 SUNDAY

Make a delicious, light smoked mackerel pâté
by whizzing in a food processor with crème fraiche,
cream cheese and a squeeze of lemon juice.

June

I love this time of year, as the weather warms and we can dine alfresco. There is nothing better on a balmy summer's evening than a mouth-watering salad full of seasonal ingredients like rocket, tomatoes, sugar snap peas and basil.

JUNE 2008

02 MONDAY Bank Holiday, R. of Ireland

03 TUESDAY ● New Moon

04 WEDNESDAY

05 THURSDAY

06 FRIDAY

07 SATURDAY

08 SUNDAY

WK	M	T	W	T	F	S	S
22							1
23	2	3	4	5	6	7	8
24	9	10	11	12	13	14	15
25	16	17	18	19	20	21	22
26	23	24	25	26	27	28	29
27	30						

JUNE 2008

09 MONDAY

10 TUESDAY

11 WEDNESDAY

12 THURSDAY

13 FRIDAY

14 SATURDAY

15 SUNDAY Father's Day, UK, Canada & USA

For a beautiful, light summer Sunday roast, stuff
a chicken with quartered lemons and sprigs of thyme
and serve with a leafy salad.

Carrageen Moss Pudding with Poached Rhubarb

This delicate, summery dessert is a Ballymaloe favourite. Serve with poached fruit such as rhubarb, apricots or gooseberries.

SERVES 4–6

7g (¼oz or 1 fistful carrageen – don't use too much
    or it will be too set and strong in flavour)
900ml (1½ pints) milk
50g (2oz) caster sugar
1 egg, separated
1 tsp vanilla extract

FOR THE POACHED RHUBARB
100ml (3½fl oz) water
225g (8oz) sugar
450g (1lb) rhubarb, cut into 2cm (¾in) chunks
    (discard the base and top of the stalks)

1. Soak the carrageen in tepid water for 10 minutes, then drain and place in a saucepan with the milk. Bring to the boil, then simmer over a very low heat for 20 minutes.

2. Pour the milk through a sieve into a bowl. The carrageen will now be swollen and resembling a jellyfish, so push the jelly through the sieve into the milk. Discard the carrageen. Whisk in the sugar, egg yolk and vanilla extract.

3. Whisk the egg white until stiff and gently stir it into the milk – it will rise to give the pudding a light, fluffy top. Pour into one large bowl or into individual cups or glasses. Cover and place in the fridge for 1–2 hours to set.

4. To poach the rhubarb, place the water and sugar in a saucepan, stir and bring to the boil. Add the rhubarb, cover, bring to the boil and simmer for exactly 1 minute. Turn off the heat and allow the rhubarb to continue cooking in the covered saucepan until almost cool. Transfer to a bowl to finish cooling.

5. Serve the rhubarb on top of or with the carrageen moss pudding.

16 MONDAY

17 TUESDAY

18 WEDNESDAY ○ Full Moon

19 THURSDAY

20 FRIDAY

21 SATURDAY Longest Day

22 SUNDAY

WK	M	T	W	T	F	S	S
22							1
23	2	3	4	5	6	7	8
24	9	10	11	12	13	14	15
25	16	17	18	19	20	21	22
26	23	24	25	26	27	28	29
27	30						

JUNE 2008

23 MONDAY

24 TUESDAY

25 WEDNESDAY

26 THURSDAY

27 FRIDAY

28 SATURDAY

29 SUNDAY

Try drizzling strawberries with lime juice and
honey, or a dash of balsamic vinegar and serve
with mascarpone for an alfresco summer dessert.

July

We always have an abundance of fruits to enjoy throughout the summer months. It's the perfect excuse to make a divine summer berry pudding, or to roast fruits like nectarines and plums wrapped in foil on the barbeque.

30 MONDAY

01 TUESDAY Canada Day, Canada

02 WEDNESDAY

03 THURSDAY ● New Moon

04 FRIDAY Independence Day, USA

05 SATURDAY

06 SUNDAY

WK	M	T	W	T	F	S	S
27		1	2	3	4	5	6
28	7	8	9	10	11	12	13
29	14	15	16	17	18	19	20
30	21	22	23	24	24	26	27
31	28	29	30	31			

07 MONDAY

08 TUESDAY

09 WEDNESDAY

10 THURSDAY

11 FRIDAY

12 SATURDAY

13 SUNDAY

Enjoy wild salmon while it is in season, either serve
hot with hollandaise sauce, or room temperature with
fresh herb mayonnaise.

JULY 2008

14 **MONDAY** Bank Holiday, N. Ireland

15 **TUESDAY**

16 **WEDNESDAY**

17 **THURSDAY**

18 **FRIDAY** ○ Full Moon

19 **SATURDAY**

20 **SUNDAY**

Beef and Rocket Wraps

I often find myself craving one of these wraps. Great for picnics and barbeques!

SERVES 4

350g (12oz) sirloin of beef, cut into strips 5mm (¼in) thick
Freshly ground black pepper
4 tbsp mayonnaise
1 generous tbsp chopped fresh tarragon
1 level tbsp Dijon mustard
A drizzle of olive oil
4 wheat flour tortillas
4 handfuls of rocket
4 tbsp finely grated Parmesan cheese
2 tbsp chopped black olives

1. Heat up a frying pan. While the pan is heating, sprinkle the beef with pepper and mix the mayonnaise with the chopped tarragon and the Dijon mustard.
2. Place the beef on the hot pan with a drizzle of olive oil and cook on both sides for a minute or two, slightly longer if you want it well cooked.
3. When the beef is cooked, turn off the heat and allow it to sit and rest for a minute.
4. Spread 1 tbsp tarragon mayonnaise on each torilla, then scatter with the rocket. Arrange the beef over the rocket and sprinkle with the Parmesan and olives. Roll up and eat straight away.

JULY 2008

21 MONDAY

22 TUESDAY

23 WEDNESDAY

24 THURSDAY

25 FRIDAY

26 SATURDAY

27 SUNDAY

WK	M	T	W	T	F	S	S
27		1	2	3	4	5	6
28	7	8	9	10	11	12	13
29	14	15	16	17	18	19	20
30	21	22	23	24	24	26	27
31	28	29	30	31			

28 **MONDAY**

29 **TUESDAY**

30 **WEDNESDAY**

31 **THURSDAY**

01 FRIDAY ● New Moon

02 SATURDAY

03 SUNDAY

♡ When boiling green vegetables, keep the fresh green
colour by cooking with the lid off at a high heat
for just a few minutes.

August

Sweetcorn is just delightful this time of the year. Either grill on the barbeque or wrap in foil first to keep it plump and juicy. Then simply sprinkle with sea salt, or dip in crème frâiche for a delectable summer supper.

AUGUST 2008

04 MONDAY Bank Holiday, Scotland & R. of Ireland

05 TUESDAY

06 WEDNESDAY

07 THURSDAY

08 FRIDAY

09 SATURDAY

10 SUNDAY

WK	M	T	W	T	F	S	S
31					1	2	3
32	4	5	6	7	8	9	10
33	11	12	13	14	15	16	17
34	18	19	20	21	22	23	24
35	25	26	27	28	29	30	31

11 **MONDAY**

12 **TUESDAY**

13 **WEDNESDAY**

14 **THURSDAY**

15 **FRIDAY**

16 **SATURDAY** ○ Full Moon

17 **SUNDAY**

♡ **Soak tomatoes in boiling water for 10 seconds to remove the skins. Perfect for pasta sauces with lots of lovely fresh basil.**

Chicken and Avocado Salad with Anchovy Mayonnaise

I love this salad, the dressing is very similar to a Caesar Salad dressing and the anchovies add a tasty kick. This is a great main course for lunch or for summer alfresco dining.

SERVES 4–6

FOR THE SALAD:
1 head of cos (romaine) lettuce
1 large or 2 small chicken breasts
A drizzle of olive oil
Sea salt and pepper
3 slices of white bread, crusts
  removed, cut into 2cm cubes
3 tbsp olive oil

TO SERVE:
1 avocado, peeled, stone removed,
 and sliced or chopped
25g (1 oz) coarsely grated Parmesan
  cheese

FOR THE DRESSING:
1 small egg yolk
8 anchovies, finely chopped
1 small clove of crushed or finely
  grated garlic
1/4 tsp English mustard
1 tbsp lemon juice
1 tsp Worcestershire sauce
1/2 – 1 tsp Tabasco sauce
25ml (1fl oz) olive oil
50ml (1¾fl oz) sunflower oil
2 tbsp water

1. Preheat the oven to 220°C (425°F) Gas Mark 7.
2. Wash the lettuce and place in a bowl in the fridge until ready for use (place a wet piece of kitchen paper over the leaves to keep them crisp).
3. Drizzle the chicken breasts with a little olive oil, and sprinkle with sea salt and pepper. Place on a baking tray and cook in the preheated oven for 15–20 minutes, until cooked through.
4. While the chicken is cooking toss the cubes of bread with the 3 tbsp olive oil, and place in a single layer on an ovenproof plate next to the chicken, cook for 4 or 5 minutes until golden, then place the croûtons on kitchen paper to drain.
5. Next, make the dressing. Place the egg yolk in a bowl (or in the bowl of a small food processor) with the chopped anchovies, garlic, mustard, lemon juice, Worcestershire sauce and the Tabasco sauce. Whisk everything together, then add the olive and sunflower oils very

slowly whisking all the time, until all the oil is added and the mixture is emulsified. Whisk in the water to thin it slightly. Season to taste.

6. When the chicken has cooled slightly, cut it into slices at an angle. Take the lettuce leaves out of the fridge, add the croûtons, chicken and avocado. Add enough dressing to coat the leaves lightly, sprinkle with the grated parmesan cheese, and serve.

AUGUST 2008

18 MONDAY

19 TUESDAY

20 WEDNESDAY

21 THURSDAY

22 FRIDAY

23 SATURDAY

24 SUNDAY

WK	M	T	W	T	F	S	S
31					1	2	3
32	4	5	6	7	8	9	10
33	11	12	13	14	15	16	17
34	18	19	20	21	22	23	24
35	25	26	27	28	29	30	31

AUGUST 2008

25 **MONDAY** Late Summer Holiday, UK (not Scotland)

26 TUESDAY

27 WEDNESDAY

28 THURSDAY

29 FRIDAY

30 **SATURDAY** ◐ New Moon

31 SUNDAY

♡ **Marinate lamb or chicken with yoghurt, garlic, ground cumin and coriander for a simple, summery barbecue dish.**

September

September is a month of abundance, with so many delicious fruits and vegetables becoming ripe and ready to eat. It's a great time to use surplus fruit in jams, chutneys and pickles. Take the time to enjoy the last of the summer sunshine and go blackberry picking with your children.

SEPTEMBER 2008

01 MONDAY

02 TUESDAY

03 WEDNESDAY

04 THURSDAY

05 FRIDAY

06 SATURDAY

07 SUNDAY

WK	M	T	W	T	F	S	S
36	1	2	3	4	5	6	7
37	8	9	10	11	12	13	14
38	15	16	17	18	19	20	21
39	22	23	24	25	26	27	28
40	29	30					

08 MONDAY

09 TUESDAY

10 WEDNESDAY

11 THURSDAY

12 FRIDAY

13 SATURDAY

14 SUNDAY

♡ Autumn raspberries are so tasty in a fresh fruit
smoothie, with meringues and cream, or whizzed up
and added to sparkling wine for a fun summer cocktail.

Irish Apple Cake

This wonderful cake is a delicious way to make the most of the autumn apples. My husband's grandmother, Myrtle Allen, has been making this for many years, and it is still made today at Ballymaloe.

SERVES 4–6
225g (8oz) plain white flour
1/2 tsp baking powder
100g (4oz) butter
100g (4oz) sugar, plus 2 tbsp
1 egg, beaten
100ml (3¹/2fl oz) milk (approximately)
1 large cooking apple, about 300g (11oz) in weight
1 level tsp cinnamon

TO SERVE
Softly whipped cream

1. Preheat the oven to 180°C (350°F), Gas Mark 4.
2. Mix the flour with the baking powder. Rub in the butter with your fingertips until the texture resembles breadcrumbs. Add the sugar, beaten egg and enough milk to form a soft dough. Pat out one half of the dough onto a greased 25cm (10in) ovenproof plate (don't worry – it is supposed to be very wet).
3. Peel, core and chop up the apple into 2cm (³/4in) squared pieces, place on the dough and sprinkle with 1 tbsp sugar and the tsp of cinnamon. Gently spoon out the remaining dough on top of the apples to cover them completely. Sprinkle with the remaining sugar and cut a slit through the middle of the lid.
4. Bake for 40–50 minutes until golden and crunchy on the outside (the apples should be soft on the inside). Serve with softly whipped cream.

Rachel's handy tip: If the butter is cold (i.e. taken from the fridge), grate it into the flour and it will rub in within a couple of seconds.

SEPTEMBER 2008

15 **MONDAY** ○ Full Moon

16 **TUESDAY**

17 **WEDNESDAY**

18 **THURSDAY**

19 **FRIDAY**

20 **SATURDAY**

21 **SUNDAY**

WK	M	T	W	T	F	S	S
36	1	2	3	4	5	6	7
37	8	9	10	11	12	13	14
38	15	16	17	18	19	20	21
39	22	23	24	25	26	27	28
40	29	30					

22 MONDAY

23 TUESDAY

24 WEDNESDAY

25 THURSDAY

26 FRIDAY

27 SATURDAY

28 SUNDAY

To remove the strong smell of certain foods like
smoked salmon and garlic from your hands, rub
your hands around a stainless steel bowl or sink
to neutralise the smell.

October

Pumpkins are my favourite autumnal treat. They're so colourful and versatile. They taste fantastic roasted or as a filling in pasta, pies and soups. Of course, you can also have endless enjoyment making Halloween Jack O' Lanterns!

SEPTEMBER OCTOBER 2008

29 MONDAY ● New Moon

30 TUESDAY

01 WEDNESDAY National Day, Hong Kong

02 THURSDAY

03 FRIDAY

04 SATURDAY

05 SUNDAY

WK	M	T	W	T	F	S	S
40			1	2	3	4	5
41	6	7	8	9	10	11	12
42	13	14	15	16	17	18	19
43	20	21	22	23	24	24	26
44	27	28	29	30	31		

OCTOBER 2008

06 MONDAY

07 TUESDAY

08 WEDNESDAY

09 THURSDAY

10 FRIDAY

11 SATURDAY

12 SUNDAY

♡ Add a glass of red wine to a hearty beef or lamb
stew for a warming autumnal supper.

OCTOBER 2008

13 MONDAY

14 TUESDAY ○ Full Moon

15 WEDNESDAY

16 THURSDAY

17 FRIDAY

18 SATURDAY

19 SUNDAY

Chocolate Cup Cakes

These make great Halloween treats. Why not get creative with festive decorations!

MAKES 12

50g (2oz) dark chocolate
100g (4oz) butter, softened
100g (4oz) soft light brown sugar
2 eggs, slightly beaten
100g (4oz) plain flour
1/2 tsp cream of tartar
1/4 tsp bicarbonate of soda
1 tbsp cocoa power

FOR THE ICING

50g (2oz) butter
2 tbsp single cream
150g (5oz) icing sugar
40g (1³/₄oz) cocoa powder

1. Preheat the oven to 180°C (350°F), Gas mark 4. Fill a bun tray with 12 paper bun cases or small muffin cases.

2. Melt the chocolate in a bowl sitting over simmering water. Set aside and allow to cool slightly. In a large bowl, cream the butter and sugar until pale and light, and then stir in the chocolate. Beat in the eggs gradually, then sift in the flour, cream of tartar, bicarbonate of soda and the cocoa powder. Stir gently to mix. Divide the mixture between the paper cases and bake in the oven for 14–16 minutes or until almost firm in the centre. Cool on a wire rack.

3. Meanwhile, make the chocolate icing. Melt the butter and cream together in a bowl sitting over simmering water. Sift in the icing sugar and cocoa powder and mix. It should be of spreading consistency; if it's too wet, add another 25g (1oz) icing sugar. Spread generously onto the cooled cupcakes.

OCTOBER 2008

20 MONDAY

21 TUESDAY

22 WEDNESDAY

23 THURSDAY

24 FRIDAY

25 SATURDAY

26 SUNDAY British Summer Time ends

WK	M	T	W	T	F	S	S
40			1	2	3	4	5
41	6	7	8	9	10	11	12
42	13	14	15	16	17	18	19
43	20	21	22	23	24	24	26
44	27	28	29	30	31		

OCTOBER NOVEMBER 2008

27 **MONDAY** Bank Holiday, R. of Ireland

28 **TUESDAY** ● New Moon

29 **WEDNESDAY**

30 **THURSDAY**

31 **FRIDAY** Halloween

01 **SATURDAY**

02 **SUNDAY**

♡ **Pick up some seasonal wild mushrooms at your local farmers' market, sauté in a little butter or olive oil and add to pasta sauces and risotto.**

November

Cook up a hearty soup with nourishing seasonal veg like potato and parsnip. Serve with a hunk of warm, crusty granary bread. It's my favourite cold-weather warmer and the best tonic for those November sniffles.

NOVEMBER 2008

03 **MONDAY**

04 **TUESDAY**

05 **WEDNESDAY**

06 **THURSDAY**

07 **FRIDAY**

08 **SATURDAY**

09 **SUNDAY** Remembrance Sunday, UK

WK	M	T	W	T	F	S	S
44						1	2
45	3	4	5	6	7	8	9
46	10	11	12	13	14	15	16
47	17	18	19	20	21	22	23
48	24	25	26	27	28	29	30

10 MONDAY

11 TUESDAY

12 WEDNESDAY

13 THURSDAY ○ Full Moon

14 FRIDAY

15 SATURDAY

16 SUNDAY

♡ Make lots of soups, stews and tagines and freeze in
small containers for a nutritious, convenient meal on
those cold winter evenings.

The Weekend Breakfast Bap with Quick Hollandaise Sauce

This is a great way to start a lazy Sunday when it's raining outside and you crave some comfort food!

SERVES 4

4 flat mushrooms
15g (½oz) butter, cut into 4 pieces
Salt and freshly ground black pepper
2 tsp chopped fresh parsley
12 small rashers of good-quality streaky bacon
4 baps (flattish yeast rolls, like burger buns)

EASY HOLLANDAISE SAUCE

1 large egg yolk
50g (2oz) butter, cut into cubes
Splash of lemon juice

1. Preheat the oven to 200°C (400°F), Gas mark 6.
2. Remove the stalks from the mushrooms and discard. Place the mushrooms, stalk side up, on a baking tray, place the butter in the centre of each mushroom, season with salt and pepper and sprinkle with the chopped parsley. Place in the oven and cook for 10 minutes.
3. While the mushrooms are cooking, grill the streaky bacon until crisp and golden. Keep warm.
4. To make the Hollandaise sauce, place the egg yolk in a heatproof glass bowl. Heat the butter in a saucepan until foaming, then pour gradually onto the yolk, whisking all the time. Add the lemon juice, then pour into a heatproof measuring jug. Half-fill a saucepan with hot water from the kettle and place the jug of hollandaise in the saucepan to keep warm. When the water cools, place the saucepan on a gentle heat but do not let the water boil for too long or the sauce will scramble. Keep the sauce warm while you are waiting to serve.
5. Split the baps in half and toast lightly. To assemble, place the bottom of each bap on a warm plate and place a warm cooked mushroom on top, then add 3 rashers of streaky bacon before drizzling with warm hollandaise sauce. Top with the remaining bap half and serve.

NOVEMBER 2008

17 **MONDAY**

18 **TUESDAY**

19 **WEDNESDAY**

20 **THURSDAY**

21 **FRIDAY**

22 **SATURDAY**

23 **SUNDAY**

WK	M	T	W	T	F	S	S
44						1	2
45	3	4	5	6	7	8	9
46	10	11	12	13	14	15	16
47	17	18	19	20	21	22	23
48	24	25	26	27	28	29	30

24 MONDAY

25 TUESDAY

26 WEDNESDAY

27 THURSDAY ● New Moon | Thanksgiving Day, USA

28 FRIDAY

29 SATURDAY

30 SUNDAY St. Andrew's Day

♡ **Try making Brussels sprout purée by whizzing with
a dash of cream, or enjoy a Brussels sprout soup served
with cheese on toast.**

December

It's the month to indulge and how better than carving up a big tender turkey to enjoy with your loved ones? Create a delicious rich and textured stuffing with bacon and chestnuts.

DECEMBER 2008

01 MONDAY

02 TUESDAY

03 WEDNESDAY

04 THURSDAY

05 FRIDAY

06 SATURDAY

07 SUNDAY

WK	M	T	W	T	F	S	S
49	1	2	3	4	5	6	7
50	8	9	10	11	12	13	14
51	15	16	17	18	19	20	21
52	22	23	24	24	26	27	28
1	29	30	31				

08 MONDAY

09 TUESDAY

10 WEDNESDAY

11 THURSDAY

12 FRIDAY ○ Full Moon

13 SATURDAY

14 SUNDAY

♡ When making mulled wine, serve some
with apple juice in place of red wine for a warming
non-alcoholic festive drink.

15 MONDAY

16 TUESDAY

17 WEDNESDAY

18 THURSDAY

19 FRIDAY

20 SATURDAY

21 SUNDAY Shortest Day

Chicken Casserole with Chorizo, Tomatoes and Beans

This warming casserole is perfect for the winter weather, and the healthy ingredients are a welcome contrast to all that heavy seasonal food!

SERVES 6–8

1 large chicken, approximately 2.5kg (5½lb) – 3.3kg (7¼lb) cut into pieces
2tb sp olive oil
125g (5oz) chorizo, cut into 8mm (³⁄₈in) slices
2 x 400g tins of chopped tomatoes
5 cloves of garlic, peeled and left whole
Salt, freshly ground black pepper and sugar
200g (7oz) dried haricot beans (or 2 x 400g tins of pre-cooked beans, drained)
Squeeze of lemon juice

1. If using dried beans, soak them in cold water for at least 6 hours. Then drain, cover with fresh cold water and cook. Place the drained beans in a saucepan and cover generously with cold water. Don't add any salt as this will toughen the skins. Bring to the boil and simmer for 30–45 minutes. Remember to keep testing them – when they are cooked they will be soft all the way through.

2. Brown the chicken in a flameproof casserole with the 2tb sp of olive oil. Add the slices of chorizo, tomatoes and garlic. Season with salt, pepper and 1 or 2 good pinches of sugar. Bring up to the boil, cover with a lid and cook (on top of hob or in an oven pre-heated to 180°C/350°F), Gas mark 4, for 30 minutes until the chicken is cooked.

3. Remove from the oven and add the drained beans (freshly cooked or tinned) and simmer for another 5 minutes. Season to taste, adding a squeeze of lemon juice if necessary. Serve with orzo (a type of barley), boiled rice or pilaff rice.

DECEMBER 2008

22 MONDAY

23 TUESDAY

24 WEDNESDAY

25 THURSDAY Christmas Day

26 FRIDAY Boxing Day

27 SATURDAY ● New Moon

28 SUNDAY

WK	M	T	W	T	F	S	S
49	1	2	3	4	5	6	7
50	8	9	10	11	12	13	14
51	15	16	17	18	19	20	21
52	22	23	24	24	26	27	28
1	29	30	31				

29 MONDAY

30 TUESDAY

31 WEDNESDAY

01 THURSDAY

02 FRIDAY

03 SATURDAY

04 SUNDAY

♡ Add a touch of Christmas to your dessert by including mincemeat in an apple pie, crumble or fruit muffin.

Recipe notes:

Recipe notes:

Recipe notes:

Addresses:

Addresses:

Important dates in 2008

01	JANUARY	New Year's Day
14	FEBRUARY	St. Valentine's Day
01	MARCH	St. David's Day
02	MARCH	Mothering Sunday
10	MARCH	Commonwealth Day
17	MARCH	St. Patrick's Day
21	MARCH	Good Friday
24	MARCH	Easter Monday
30	MARCH	British Summer Time Begins
23	APRIL	St. George's Day
05	MAY	May Day Holiday, UK & R. of Ireland
26	MAY	Bank Holiday, UK
02	JUNE	Bank Holiday, R. of Ireland
15	JUNE	Father's Day, UK, Canada & USA
21	JUNE	Longest Day
14	JULY	Bank Holiday, N. Ireland
04	AUGUST	Bank Holiday, Scotland & R. of Ireland
25	AUGUST	Bank Holiday (not Scotland)
26	OCTOBER	British Summer Time Ends
27	OCTOBER	Bank Holiday, R. of Ireland
31	OCTOBER	Halloween
09	NOVEMBER	Remembrance Sunday, UK
30	NOVEMBER	St. Andrew's Day
21	DECEMBER	Shortest Day
25	DECEMBER	Christmas Day
26	DECEMBER	Boxing Day

2009 at a glance

	January	February	March	April	May	June
Mon						1
Tue						2
Wed				1		3
Thur	1			2		4
Fri	2			3	1	5
Sat	3			4	2	6
Sun	4	1	1	5	3	7
Mon	5	2	2	6	4	8
Tue	6	3	3	7	5	9
Wed	7	4	4	8	6	10
Thur	8	5	5	9	7	11
Fri	9	6	6	10	8	12
Sat	10	7	7	11	9	13
Sun	11	8	8	12	10	14
Mon	12	9	9	13	11	15
Tue	13	10	10	14	12	16
Wed	14	11	11	15	13	17
Thur	15	12	12	16	14	18
Fri	16	13	13	17	15	19
Sat	17	14	14	18	16	20
Sun	18	15	15	19	17	21
Mon	19	16	16	20	18	22
Tue	20	17	17	21	19	23
Wed	21	18	18	22	20	24
Thur	22	19	19	23	21	25
Fri	23	20	20	24	22	26
Sat	24	21	21	25	23	27
Sun	25	22	22	26	24	28
Mon	26	23	23	27	25	29
Tue	27	24	24	28	26	30
Wed	28	25	25	29	27	
Thur	29	26	26	30	28	
Fri	30	27	27		29	
Sat	31	28	28		30	
Sun			29		31	
Mon			30			
Tue			31			

July	August	September	October	November	December	
						Mon
		1			1	Tue
1		2			2	Wed
2		3	1		3	Thur
3		4	2		4	Fri
4	1	5	3		5	Sat
5	2	6	4	1	6	Sun
6	3	7	5	2	7	Mon
7	4	8	6	3	8	Tue
8	5	9	7	4	9	Wed
9	6	10	8	5	10	Thur
10	7	11	9	6	11	Fri
11	8	12	10	7	12	Sat
12	9	13	11	8	13	Sun
13	10	14	12	9	14	Mon
14	11	15	13	10	15	Tue
15	12	16	14	11	16	Wed
16	13	17	15	12	17	Thur
17	14	18	16	13	18	Fri
18	15	19	17	14	19	Sat
19	16	20	18	15	20	Sun
20	17	21	19	16	21	Mon
21	18	22	20	17	22	Tue
22	19	23	21	18	23	Wed
23	20	24	22	19	24	Thur
24	21	25	23	20	25	Fri
25	22	26	24	21	26	Sat
26	23	27	25	22	27	Sun
27	24	28	26	23	28	Mon
28	25	29	27	24	29	Tue
29	26	30	28	25	30	Wed
30	27		29	26	31	Thur
31	28		30	27		Fri
	29		31	28		Sat
	30			29		Sun
	31			30		Mon
						Tue

First published in 2007 by Collins,
An imprint of HarperCollins Publishers Ltd.
77–85 Fulham Palace Road, London W6 8JB

The Collins website address is: www.collins.co.uk

Collins is a registered trademark of HarperCollins
Publishers Ltd.

10 09 08 07

8 7 6 5 4 3 2 1

A catalogue record for this book is available from
the British Library.

ISBN 978-0-00-725932-8

Editorial Director: Jenny Heller
Editor: Kerenza Swift
Recipes Copy Editor: Gillian Haslam
Design: Smith & Gilmour, London
Photography (see above): Georgia Glynn Smith;
Cristian Barnett
Props Stylist: Róisín Nield
Food Stylist: Annie Nichols

Colour reproduction by Colourscan, Singapore
Printed and bound by Lego, Italy

Temperature conversion chart

Conventional oven	Fan oven	Fahrenheit	Gas mark	Aga 2 oven	Aga 3 & 4 oven
150°C	130°C	300°F	2	Simmering oven	Simmering oven
170°C	150°C	325°F	3	Grid shelf on floor of roasting oven and cold plain shelf above	Grid shelf on floor of baking oven
180°C	160°C	350°F	4	Grid shelf on floor of roasting oven and cold plain shelf above	Lowest runner of baking oven
190°C	170°C	375°F	5	Grid shelf on floor of roasting oven	Top of baking oven
200°C	180°C	400°F	6	Lowest set of runners in roasting oven	Lowest set of runners in roasting oven
220°C	200°C	425°F	7	3rd or 4th set of runners in roasting oven	3rd or 4th set of runners in roasting oven
230°C	210°C	450°F	8	Middle roasting oven	Middle roasting oven
240°C	220°C	475°F	9	Roasting oven	Roasting oven